Australia's PARROTS

Galahs, *Cacatua roseicapilla* (see page 13).

Australia's
PARROTS

Above: Sulphur-crested cockatoo, *Cacatua galerita* (see page 27).
Left: The eclectus parrot, *Eclectus roratus* (see page 10).

Photography by Ken Stepnell
&
Text by Jane Dalby

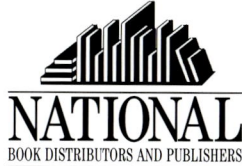

NATIONAL
BOOK DISTRIBUTORS AND PUBLISHERS

Ken Stepnell, renowned as one of Australia's leading photographers of our natural wonders, travels over 100 000 kilometres annually continually searching for new subjects to enhance his superb photographic library.

His eye for detail has enabled readers to appreciate the beauty and variety of our natural resources through many publications. His photographs show the delicate balance of nature and the need to preserve our heritage.

His other books include *Australian Birds*, *Australia's Native Flowers* and *Australia's Animals*.

Jane Dalby was encouraged to take an interest in natural history by her parents and grandparents. She obtained a BA in Biology and Ecology from Macquarie University. She is now a Technical Officer at the National Herbarium at the Botanic Gardens, Sydney, New South Wales. This involves looking after the collection of dried plants used in research and identification.

Her great interest in birds has developed over the last four or five years and has led to an extensive study of their habits and features. Her first book *Australian Birds* was published in 1986.

Above: Gang gang cockatoos, *Callocephalon fimbriatum* (see page 14).

Front cover: Major Mitchell cockatoo, *Cacatua leadbeateri* (see pages 28-9).
Back cover: Princess parrot, *Polytelis alexandrae* (see pages 37-8).

Published by National Book Distributors and Publishers
3/2 Aquatic Drive, Frenchs Forest, NSW 2086
First edition 1988
Reprinted 1989, 1993, 1994, 1996
© Photographs Ken Stepnell 1988
© Text Jane Dalby 1988
Printed in Singapore by Kyodo Printing Co (S'pore) Pte Ltd
Typesetting processed by Deblaere Typesetting Pty Ltd

All rights reserved. No part of this publication may be reproduced, stored in a retrieval system, or transmitted, in any form or by any means, electronic, mechanical, photocopying, recording or otherwise, without the prior permission in writing of the publisher.

National Library of Australia
Cataloguing-in-Publication data

Stepnell, Kenneth, 1931-
  Australia's parrots.

Includes index.
ISBN 1 86302 288 0.

1. Parrots. 2. Birds – Australia. 3. Parrots – Pictorial works. 4. Birds – Australia – Pictorial works. I. Dalby, Jane, 1945- II. Title.

598.710994

AUSTRALIAN PARROTS

Parrots, lorikeets and cockatoos belong to a most distinctive and easily recognisable group of birds, the order Psittaciformes, whose nearest relatives are believed to be the pigeons and doves.

Parrots are known to have been tamed and taught to mimic human speech since long before the time of Christ. Today, such birds as the South American macaws, African grey and peach-faced parrots, and of course many Australian cockatoos and parrots, are commonly kept as pets and aviary birds.

In Australia, a number of native species such as galahs, rosellas and lorikeets are also familiar town birds, frequenting urban bushland, parks and private gardens.

Today, about 330 species of parrot exist worldwide, the majority occurring in the southern hemisphere. Although the greatest number of species are to be found in the tropics, a significant number occur in the subtropical and temperate zones as well. The South American continent boasts the greatest number of species, although the parrots of this region are rather uniform in type. While fewer species occur in Australasia, parrots are well represented there, having evolved into a remarkable diversity of forms. Two striking groups, the lorikeets and the cockatoos, as well as a number of other species, are restricted to the region. Relatively few species of parrot are native to Africa, Asia and North America.

Australia, which is home to over fifty species, has long been known for its parrots. Dutch navigators in the seventeenth century, having seen flocks of cockatoos on the west coast of what is now known as Western Australia, named the country 'Terra Psittacorum' (Land of Parrots).

The first known drawing of an Australian parrot was of a female-plumaged red-tailed black cockatoo, made by Sydney Parkinson in 1770, on Captain Cook's first voyage to the Pacific. A live rainbow lorikeet taken back to Europe by Sir Joseph Banks was the first Australian parrot known to have been kept in captivity.

A flock of little corellas, *Cacatua sanguinea*. Such sights as this inspired the European navigators who first saw Australia to give it the name 'Terra Psittacorum' (Land of Parrots).

A rainbow lorikeet, *Trichoglossus haemadotus*, was the first Australian parrot taken back to Europe from Australia. Joseph Banks collected rainbow lorikeets on Cook's first voyage to the Pacific.

Features of Parrots

A number of striking features contribute to the characteristic appearance of parrots as a group. These include their often brilliant plumage colours, the naked or feathered cere, which bears the nostrils, the hooked bill and muscular tongue, and the zygodactylous feet, with two toes pointing forward and two backward.

Bill and Tongue

The strong hooked bill is one of the most easily recognisable features of all parrots. The bill grows continuously, at the same time being constantly worn away with use. Parrots use their bills not only for the obvious purposes of obtaining and breaking up food and for grooming, but also as an extra limb when climbing.

The upper mandible of most birds is attached directly to the skull and is immoveable from its fixed position. Parrots, however, have a complex hinge-like arrangement attaching the upper mandible to the skull. This gives them the capacity to open the beak wide and to exert considerable force with it. Anyone who has been bitten by a parrot will be able to vouch for the power of its bite! On the other hand, the bill can be used very gently when required, for example, for delicate tasks such as preening.

The crushing ability of the bill is used to open hard and woody fruits to extract the seeds which are a major component of the diet of most species. Other uses of the bill include removing insect larvae from galls or from under bark, and digging roots, corms etc. from the soil.

While the powerful hooked bill of the long-billed corella, *Cacatua tenuirostris*, is adapted for crushing woody fruits and for digging for bulbs in the soil, it is also needed for delicate tasks such as grooming.

Some species have evolved modifications of the bill which are related to the collection of particular foods. Long-billed corellas, for example, have a long upper mandible which is admirably suited for digging in the soil for bulbs and corms. Red-capped parrots also have an elongated upper mandible, which is adapted for extracting seed from the woody fruits of eucalypts, particularly those of the marri, a tree particularly favoured by this species.

The narrow protruding bills of lorikeets are adapted for probing blossom. In addition, the lorikeet group have evolved what is known as a 'brush' tongue. Numerous papillae at the tip of the tongue, which become erect during feeding, are an adaptation for taking up pollen and nectar from flowers. A similar tongue adaptation has evolved independently in the swift parrot, another specialist nectar and pollen feeder which is more closely related to the rosellas and bluebonnets than to the lorikeets.

By contrast, the cockatoos and other parrots have a thick and muscular though flexible tongue. They use the tongue, in conjunction with the beak, for manipulating and husking seeds, fruits and other food items.

Feet

Parrots have strong, short legs and feet with two toes pointing forward and two back. This arrangement enables them both to walk well on the ground, and also, often aided by the bill, to climb easily. In some species, for example, cockatoos and rosellas, the feet are often used, in conjunction with the bill and tongue, for holding and manipulating food. Preening and scratching are other functions requiring use of the feet.

Some parrot species, such as the sulphur-crested cockatoo, *Cacatua galerita*, are able to use a foot for holding food up to the bill while feeding.

In spite of the brilliant colours of birds such as this golden-mantled rosella, *Platycercus eximius* subsp. *cecilae*, they can be difficult to see when in their natural forest surroundings.

Colour

Feather structure and the presence of pigments are the factors involved in producing the colours of birds' plumage. The microscopic structure of the feathers of some species causes interference or backscattering of light. Iridescent colours, which change with viewing angle, are produced by interference, while backscattering gives rise to non-iridescent colours. Other non-iridescent colours are due to the presence of pigments or to a combination of structure and pigment. The brightest Australian parrots, such as lorikeets and rosellas are coloured mainly in green, red, blue and yellow, often with greens predominating. With colourings like these, the birds often appear very conspicuous when seen outside their normal surroundings. However, their colours are usually distributed in small broken patches, rather than in large areas of one colour. Thus, in the wild they can be very difficult to see in natural surroundings such as the vegetation of forest or woodland.

Species such as Bourke's parrot and the princess parrot are less brilliant, with plumage of lovely pastel shades of pink, blue and yellow. The regent parrot and blue-winged parrot are quite cryptically coloured, being predominantly yellow-green and olive respectively.

Cockatoos do not have the iridescent colours of other groups, as they lack the feather structure which produces these colours. The body and wing plumage of most cockatoos is basically plain black or white, with splashes or flecks of colour. The two exceptions to this are the galah, which is pink and grey, and the Major Mitchell cockatoo, which is pale pink and white, with salmon underwings.

The skin of soft parts of the body may also be coloured. The ceres of adult male budgerigars, for example, are a clear, bright blue. Galahs, depending on their subspecies, have either grey or deep pink skin around the eyes. In little corellas, this area is blue.

The most striking example of pigmented skin occurs in the palm cockatoo, *Probosciger aterrimus*. These birds have a black-tipped red tongue and red facial skin, which blushes even brighter when they are excited.

Bill colours also differ between species. The bill may be horn-coloured, grey, or black, as in cockatoos, ringnecks and rosellas; bright orange or red as in some lorikeets, or coral-coloured as in the king, red-winged, superb and princess parrots.

The lovely pastel shades of Bourke's parrot, *Neophema bourkii*, are quite a contrast to the brilliant colours of many other parrots.

The bloom or bluish sheen on the feathers of this red-tailed black cockatoo, *Calyptorhynchus magnificus*, is due to the presence of a powder which is produced by the breakdown of specialised down feathers and used by the bird for grooming its plumage.

Plumage

The most important contribution to a bird's appearance is made by the plumage, differences in which play a major role in species recognition. In addition, particular feathers have become adapted for display in some species. Good examples of this are the moveable crests of the cockatoos and the cockatiel.

Down feathers, which grow thickly under the contour feathers, provide insulation by trapping air against the skin. Parrots and several other groups of birds such as herons and woodswallows have a second type of down feather, known as 'powder down'. These feathers grow throughout the bird's life. The tips break down constantly, forming a fine powder which is used for grooming the feathers. It is this powder which gives the plumage its characteristic bloom, a feature which is particularly noticeable in the black cockatoos.

Sexual Differences

In some species of parrot, such as the little corella and the rainbow lorikeet, it is not possible to tell male and female apart visually. In many cases, however, the sexes are appreciably different in appearance. Amongst Australian parrots, the most striking instance of this phenomenon, which is known as sexual dimorphism, occurs in the eclectus parrot. The male and female of this species are so different in colouring that for many years they were thought to belong to different species. The male, which has an orange bill, is green with red flanks and wing lining, while the female has a black bill and is mostly red, with blue shoulders and breast band. Other parrots exhibit sexual dimorphism to varying degrees. The sexes are easily distinguished in such species as cockateils, black cockatoos and king parrots. In others, such as varied lorikeets and the blue-winged parrot, the differences are not as marked, the male being in general more brightly coloured than the female. The least obvious differences occur in species such as the pink cockatoo and galah, in which the sexes have similar plumage, but differ in eye colour, the male's iris being deep brown and that of the female being reddish pink.

The eclectus parrot, *Eclectus roratus*, inhabits the tropical rainforests of Cape York. This bird is a male—the female has a black bill and is mostly red, with blue shoulders and breast band.

Rainforest on Fraser Island, Queensland. Forests like this support such species as the king parrot, *Alisterus scapularis*, rosellas and lorikeets.

HABITATS

Parrots are able to exploit environments which provide their basic requirements for survival — suitable food, a water supply and nesting and roosting sites.

The Australian continent, which extends from the tropics to cool temperate zones, provides a great many suitable habitats for parrots. These include monsoon forests and rainforests, various types of woodland and grassland, tree-lined watercourses, farmlands, heath, saltmarsh and mangroves, to name but a few.

Some species of parrot have the ability to make use of a number of different habitats within their range. Lorikeets, for instance, are nomadic birds of the treetops, their movements being governed largely by the flowering of their food plants. Rainbow lorikeets have an extensive range down the eastern coast of Australia, extending to Tasmania and the south-east of South Australia. They frequent habitats ranging from tropical rainforest, sclerophyll forests and savannah woodland, to scrub and timbered watercourses and mangroves.

The blue-winged parrot of south-eastern Australia and Tasmania is another species which is able to make use of a number of different habitats. It frequents open forest, forested foothills and valleys, savannah woodland and grasslands, as well as coastal heathlands, sand dunes and saltmarsh.

The galah, one of Australia's most widespread and familiar cockatoos, was originally confined to the semi-arid and arid zones, in woodland, grassland and timber along streams. Galahs have been able to take advantage of habitat changes such as the clearing of timber and planting of grain and other crops. As a result, they have extended their range and are now to be found in areas where they were previously unknown, becoming agricultural pests in some places.

Arid environments such as the area south of Marble Bar in Western Australia are visited in favourable seasons by nomadic species like the budgerigar, *Melopsittacus undulatus*.

The hooded parrot, *Psephotus chrysopterygius* subsp. *dissimilis*, which occurs in the Northern Territory, nests in a chamber excavated in a termite mound.

Termite mounds in northern Australia. Both the golden-shouldered parrot, *Psephotus chrysopterygius*, and the hooded parrot require habitat such as this to provide nesting sites.

The swift parrot, *Lathamus discolor*, has evolved a narrow protruding bill and a brush-like tongue, adaptations for obtaining nectar and pollen from flowers.

Other, more specialised species have narrower habitat requirements, which effectively restrict their ranges. Golden-shouldered and hooded parrots occur in the Northern Territory and northern Queensland respectively. Because of their requirement for termite mounds as nesting sites, they are only to be found in open wooded habitats close to grassland where there are numerous terrestrial termite mounds present.

Rock parrots, *Neophema petrophila*, inhabit the coast and offshore islands of southern and south-western Australia. They are rarely to be seen more than a few hundred metres from the sea, in coastal sand dunes, saltmarsh and mangroves, or on small rocky islands. As these parrots only breed on islands, their range is restricted by the distribution of the coastal islands.

The seldom-seen night parrot, *Geopsittacus occidentalis*, occurs only in the arid centre of the continent. It is thought to be nomadic, and has been observed in salt lake and flood plain habitats, as well as in spinifex, when abundant seeding occurs after rain.

Ground parrots, *Pezoporus wallicus*, as their name suggests, are largely terrestrial, although they are able to fly well. They are rarely seen because of their dense habitat and their tendency to fly during daylight only if flushed from cover. Their optimum habitat is diverse heathland vegetation of 0.5 m to 1.5 m in height. This environment is dominated by sedges and heaths, scattered shrubs of banksia and teatree, and small eucalypts. Because of the destruction of this type of habitat by human activities, the ground parrot now has a distribution restricted to suitable areas scattered in coastal eastern Australia, from southeast Queensland to Victoria and Tasmania, its present stronghold.

Eclectus parrots, palm cockatoos, *Probosciger aterrimus*, and red-cheeked parrots, *Geoffroyus geoffroyi*, which occur in Australia on Cape York in Queensland, are birds of tropical rainforests. They have been prevented from extending their range to more southerly rainforests by the tract of savannah woodland to the south of Coen on Cape York Peninsula.

FEEDING

Apart from the lorikeets and the swift parrot, Australian parrots are primarily seed-eaters. However, a variety of other foods may be eaten also. These include fruits of various kinds, roots and bulbs, young shoots, flowers, pollen and nectar, and insects and their larvae.

Many Australian cockatoos and parrots are now known to include insects in their diet. Different species have been observed feeding on items identified as lerps and psillids, larvae of moths and other insects, and on the eggs of ants and plague locusts.

Some species have more specialised food requirements than others. Lorikeets, for example, forage in the treetops for pollen, nectar and fruit, but also take berries, seeds, insects and larvae.

Yellow-tailed black cockatoos feed mainly on the wood-boring larvae of moths and other insects, obtaining them from dead grass-tree spikes, dead wood and from the trunks of trees including eucalypts and wattles (*Acacia*). In part of their range, these cockatoos have been observed using extraordinary foraging behaviour. The bird first locates a hole containing a larva by listening at the tree trunk. It then proceeds to make itself a perch to work from. This it does by pulling a strip of wood from the tree trunk, so that it hinges just below the insect hole. The bird then stands on this perch and sets to work to dig out the larva.

The ground parrot, which inhabits heath and sedge lands, feeds mainly on the seeds of grasses, sedges and other herbaceous plants, as well as on young shoots. Favoured foods are the seeds of buttongrass, grasses and sedges.

The red-capped parrot of south-western Australia, also appropriately known as a 'hookbill', has a narrow, protruding bill, which is specialised for extracting seeds from the large, flask-shaped fruit of the marri, *Eucalyptus calophylla*. It also feeds on the seeds of other trees, including eucalypts and casuarinas, as well as on fruits, blossom, leaf buds and insects and larvae.

Since the advent of European man, cultivated plants have become a potential food source for birds. Hence parrots have come to be regarded as pests in some areas where commercial crops such as grains, soft fruits and nuts are grown. For example, galahs, sulphur-crested cockatoos and corellas are considered pests in grain-growing areas, where they cause damage by digging up sprouting seeds, or by eating the ripening crop or bagged grain. Others, such as king parrots and rosellas, attack fruit in apple, pear and peach orchards. In maize crops, they may eat the grain in the milky stage.

The elongated mandible of the red-capped parrot, *Purpureicephalus spurius*, is adapted for extracting seed from large eucalyptus fruits, particularly those of the marri, *Eucalyptus calophylla*.

Yellow-tailed black cockatoos, *Calyptorhynchus funereus*. Wood-boring larvae of insects, extracted from trees with their formidable bills, are an important part of the diet of this species.

The galah, *Cacatua roseicapilla*, is among Australia's most common and widespread parrots. Galahs have benefited from man's activities, such as clearing of timber and the planting of grain and oilseed crops.

COMMUNICATION

Birds have complex systems for conveying messages to each other, using combinations of calls, movements and plumage display. In this way, they co-ordinate the behaviour of members of the same species in such activities as feeding, flocking, breeding and reaction to predators.

Calls

Each species has a vocabulary of calls which are used in different situations. Thus alarm calls warning of danger are loud, but not directional, so that the bird giving the call is less likely to be located by a predator. Territorial calls are also loud, but are directional, as they are intended to identify the bird's territory. Contact calls are both quiet and non-directional, serving to maintain contact between members of the group.

The calls of Australian parrots are as varied as the birds themselves. The harsh, raucous cries of some of the cockatoos and the shrill screeching of lorikeets will be known to many people. The cheerful chattering of budgerigars is also a familiar sound the world over.

Not all of Australia's parrots have shrill or raucous calls, however. Some species, such as the king parrot and the eastern rosella, have rather musical notes among their repertoire of calls. Others make sounds which are quite unusual. The feeding call of gang gang cockatoos, for example, is a soft growling, while their contact call is a curious creaking sound.

Ground parrots give an ascending series of very high-pitched whistles which may be inaudible to some people. They usually call for short periods at dawn and dusk, as they fly between their roost trees and their daytime feeding areas in the heath.

Display

Palm cockatoos have recently been observed behaving in a most remarkable manner. Within their territory, they have a number of tree hollows which they visit regularly. Near these, they display by beating on a hollow trunk or limb, producing a drumming sound. This display is of particular interest because the drumming is produced with the aid of a tool, a type of behaviour exhibited by very few animals apart from man. The 'drumstick' may be a specially prepared stick, or the large woody fruit of the 'bushman's clothespeg', *Grevillea glauca*. This is held in the foot and beaten on a hollow limb. Drumming occurs early in the morning and evening and takes place most frequently during nest preparation and in the period just before the single young leaves the nest. Its functions appear to be to proclaim territory and perhaps to maintain the pair-bond.

Amongst parrots, courtship displays are usually quite uncomplicated, involving a series of simple actions. These include bowing, drooping and flicking of the wings, tail wagging, foot raising and dilation and contraction of the pupils. As mating approaches, the birds engage in close body contact such as mutual preening and courtship feeding, where the female is fed regurgitated food by the male, in the same manner as chicks are fed by the adults.

There is a marked difference in appearance between male and female gang gang cockatoos, *Callocephalon fimbriatum*. The head and crest of the male are a clear bright red, while those of the female are grey.

The male rainbow lorikeet courts the female by moving towards her, bobbing and bowing, and then stretching to his full height with his neck arched. During this display, the pupils of his eyes continually dilate and contract, and he gives a low whistle.

Cockatoos use their moveable crests in their displays. The male Major Mitchell cockatoo, for example, struts towards the female with his lovely red, yellow and white crest raised. He bobs his head, and may also move it in a rapid 'figure of eight' action. Often he also raises his wings to display the bright salmon pink feathers underneath. The female may also raise her crest, and bow to her suitor.

During their courtship, both male and female king parrots will fluff up their head feathers, simultaneously tightening the body feathers and contracting the pupils of the eyes. The male flicks his wings rapidly, showing off their pale green stripe, and utters their contact call. The female calls intermittently and bobs her head to solicit courtship feeding, which usually follows.

Continuous chattering accompanies the courtship display of crimson rosellas. The male sits on a branch close to the female, drooping his wings to expose the raised feathers of the rump and fluffing out his breast feathers. He holds his head high and rapidly wags his fanned tail.

Tail wagging is also part of the display of the bluebonnet. Standing upright and pushing his shoulders forward, the male raises the deep blue feathers at the top of his head to form a small crest, while stretching his neck out and bobbing his head.

A male king parrot, *Alisterus scapularis*. During his courtship display, he flicks his wings rapidly to display the pale green strip on the wing to the female.

The male varied lorikeet, *Psitteuteles versicolor*, is more brightly coloured than the female. When displaying, he stretches to his full height, arching his neck and dilating his pupils, bobbing up and down while hopping towards his mate.

Gnarled old trees, full of hollows, provide nesting sites for parrots and other creatures. Destruction of these trees for agriculture and logging removes valuable habitat for many animals.

BREEDING

Most breeding takes place in spring and summer, although in arid and semi-arid regions, nesting may take place at any time, providing conditions are suitable. Species such as galahs and budgerigars are adapted to these environments and are able to respond quickly following rainfall and the ensuing abundant food supply.

Most parrots appear to remain paired for long periods, even for life, maintaining the bond outside the breeding season. The pair-bond is maintained by the constant close association of the birds as well as by mutual preening and courtship feeding.

While the majority of Australian parrots nest in hollow limbs or in tree hollows, there are several exceptions to this. The golden-shouldered and hooded parrots of northern Australia nest in termite mounds, laying their eggs in a chamber excavated at the end of a tunnel. The paradise parrot of central Queensland, *Psephotus pulcherrimus*, which is now thought to be exctinct, also nested in termite mounds.

Rock parrots nest in crevices in rocks, while the ground and night parrots, which are both largely terrestrial, build their nests in thick vegetation on the ground.

Mutual preening by this pair of cockatiels, *Nymphicus hollandicus*, helps to maintain their pair-bond.

Parrots lay white eggs, a characteristic common amongst hole-nesting birds, there being no need for camouflage where the eggs are hidden. Those species which do not nest in hollows have retained this feature.

Before the eggs are laid, the nest hole is cleaned out by the adult birds. In most cases, the only lining provided is a layer of decayed wood chips. Galahs, however, carry fresh eucalypt leaves to the nest, while palm cockatoos line the hollow with a deep layer of splintered sticks.

For most Australian parrots, the usual clutch size is two or more. Cockatoos usually lay two or three eggs, while other parrots lay up to seven or eight. Some species, such as the palm cockatoo and the gang gang cockatoo lay only one egg. White-tailed black cockatoos mostly lay two eggs, but it is unusual for both chicks to be reared.

In most Australian parrots, the female alone broods the eggs, being fed by the male by regurgitation. In a few species such as cockatiels and gang gang cockatoos, both parents share incubation.

When the chicks first hatch, they are blind and naked except for sparse down. At first they are fed by the female, but later are tended by both parents.

The newly hatched young of the ground parrot are covered with thick grey down. Recent monitoring of nest-

Provision of permanent water supplies in arid areas have benefited many birds, such as these little corellas, *Cacatua sanguinea*.

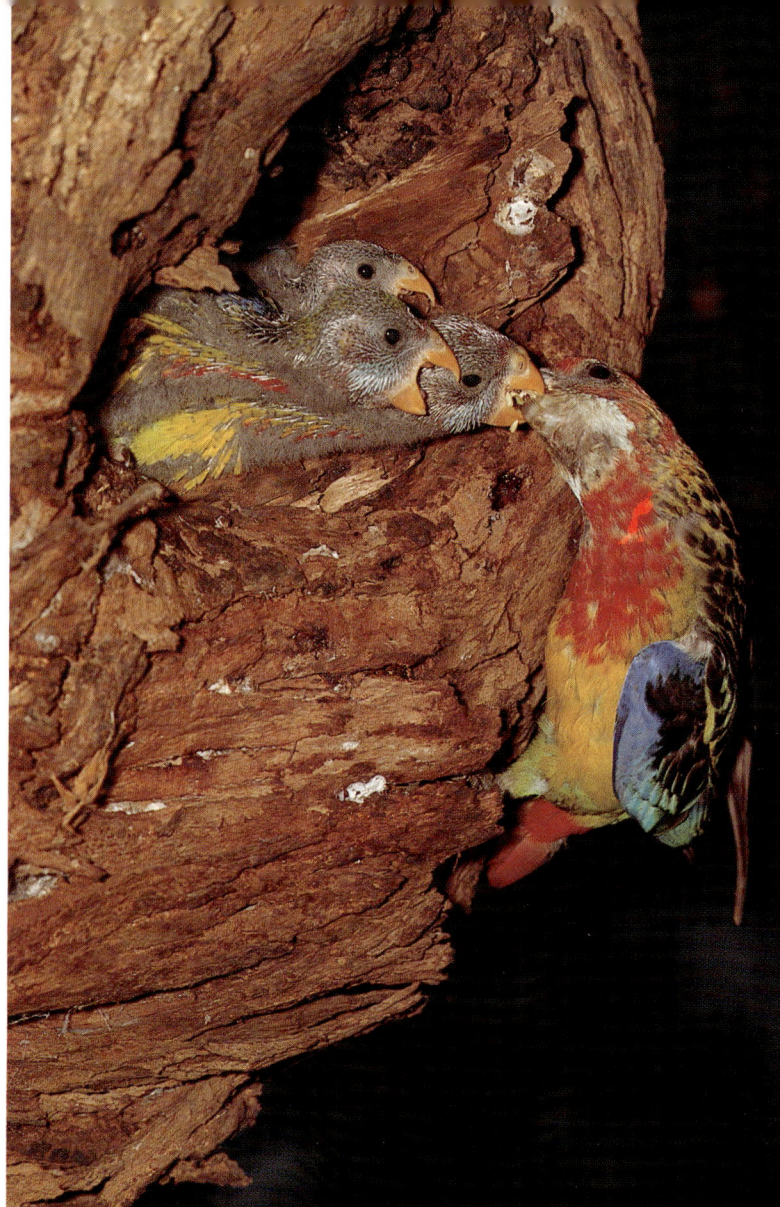

An adult golden-mantled rosella, *Platycercus eximius* subsp. *cecilae*, feeds its young in its nest hollow in a eucalypt.

ing ground parrots has revealed that while the female broods the eggs, once they are hatched, the chicks are cared for exclusively by the male.

Young birds once fledged stay with their parents for varying lengths of time. For example, juvenile galahs form wandering flocks with non-breeding adults. Young red-rumped parrots, with their parents, join feeding flocks after the breeding season. In other species such as rosellas, mulga parrots and Bourke's parrot, the adults and young remain together, forming family parties.

The beauty and diversity of Australia's parrots, lorikeets and cockatoos are admirably illustrated by the photographs in this book, which includes about four-fifths of the species which inhabit this country. While the beauty of these birds is evident in all these photographs, various aspects of their structure, habits and habitats are also illustrated.

LORIKEETS

Lorikeets are brightly coloured, noisy and fast-flying birds of the treetops. Members of this group are found only in the Papuo-Australasian region, with six species occurring in Australia. Lorikeets are often nomadic, wandering in search of pollen, nectar and fruit. Their narrow protruding bills and brush tongues are adaptations related to foraging for these foods.

Rainbow lorikeets, *Trichoglossus haemadotus*, occur in many habitats in eastern Australia from Cape York to Tasmania and the Eyre Peninsula in South Australia. They are mainly nomadic, but will remain in one place if a stable food source is available.

Lorikeets are quite readily attracted to feeding tables. Here scaly-breasted lorikeets, *Trichoglossus chlorolepidotus*, and rainbow lorikeets, *Trichoglossus haemadotus*, jostle for their share of a free meal.

Little lorikeets, *Glossopsitta pusilla*, occur in eastern and south-eastern Australia. They are strictly nomadic and are usually seen in groups of about ten birds. However they sometimes form large flocks and often feed with other lorikeets.

Adults and children alike delight in the experience of seeing rainbow lorikeets at close quarters. This child is obviously enthralled as the birds feed from a hand-held dish.

COCKATOOS

Members of this group are to be found in the Papuo-Australasian region, with eleven species occurring in Australia They are large, relatively plain-coloured birds, usually with loud voices, and are easily recognised by their characteristic mobile crest. This is usually raised just after the bird alights, during courtship, or as a sign of alarm. Cockatoos lack the feather structure which produces the iridescent colours common in other groups of parrots.

The yellow-tailed black cockatoo, *Calyptorhynchus funereus*, occurs in most types of timbered country in eastern Australia from central Queensland to eastern Victoria. This photograph illustrates the way in which cockatoos are able to use the foot for holding food up to the bill.

The male yellow-tailed black cockatoo has a black bill and a pink ring around the eye, while the female has a horn-coloured bill and a dark ring around the eye.

(Left)

The varied lorikeet, *Psitteuteles versicolor*, is the only lorikeet to have a white ring around the eye. This species occurs in the tropical lowlands of northern Australia, from the Kimberleys in Western Australia to the west of the Great Divide in northern Quensland.

Red-tailed black cockatoos, *Calyptorhynchus magnificus*, are essentially tropical birds. They occur most commonly in northern Australia, preferring open woodland and tree-lined watercourses as their usual habitats. This young male has not yet developed full adult plumage. Adult males are all black except for the red in the tail. Females have a light-coloured bill and are brownish black with numerous yellow spots on the head and wings. The underparts and tail are barred in yellow merging into orange.

(Left)

Two female white-tailed black cockatoos, *Calyptorhynchus funereus* subsp. *baudinii*, explore a hollow log. This species is found in heavily forested areas on south-western Western Australia. The seeds of eucalyptus trees and the wood-boring larvae of insects are important food items of this species. Males have a dark grey bill, dusky white ear patches and a pink ring around the eye.

Male and female gang gang cockatoos, *Callocephalon fimbriatum*, are markedly different in appearance. The male has the red head and crest.

Gang gangs are restricted to south-eastern Australia from the central coastal strip of New South Wales, through Victoria to south-eastern South Australia. They inhabit temperate forests and woodlands from the coast to the ranges. In winter they may sometimes be seen in suburban gardens and parkland.

(Right)

The galah or rose-breasted cockatoo, *Cacatua roseicapilla*, is one of our most beautiful birds. This may not always be appreciated, however, as it is also one of the most common and widespread of cockatoos. In agricultural areas, it is regarded as a pest.

Non-breeding adult galahs and juveniles form large wandering flocks. Breeding pairs are sedentary, but join loose feeding flocks in which the pairs remain together.

A flock of galahs feed on spilt grain. Although galahs feed primarily on the seeds of grasses and other plants, their diet also includes nuts, berries, green shoots and buds, roots, flowers and insect larvae.

(Right)
The sulphur-crested cockatoo, *Cacatua galerita*, is a familiar bird to Australians, in its natural range from the Kimberleys in Western Australia to Cape York Peninsula in Queensland and most of the eastern third of Australia, including Tasmania. White 'cockies' as they are affectionately known, are also familiar worldwide as pets and aviary birds.

A sulphur-crested cockatoo with crest raised gives its loud, harsh call. The crest is usually raised just after the bird alights, when it is alarmed and during territorial and courtship display.

(Right)
Major Mitchell cockatoo, *Cacatua leadbeateri*, is also popularly known by the names 'pink cockatoo' and 'wee juggler'. These lovely birds occur in woodland environments in arid and semi-arid zones in the interior of the continent.

Because of their dependence on woodland habitats, pink cockatoos have not benefited from land clearing as have other, more adaptable species. This species has been severely affected by illegal trappers and nest robbers who take them for sale as pets.

The long-billed corella, *Cacatua tenuirostris*, has a broken distribution. There are two populations, one in south-western Western Australia, and another centred on western Victoria. This species frequents grasslands and crop paddocks close to timbered watercourses and is rarely seen far from water. These birds were regarded as endangered at one time, but their numbers have recovered and they may be considered a pest in some areas.

Outside the breeding season, long-billed corellas congregate in large flocks, especially where food is plentiful. Nesting adults form small groups of about ten birds, remaining close to their nest trees. Young birds and non-breeding adults form larger foraging flocks.

THE COCKATIEL

Cockatiels, *Nymphicus hollandicus*, share a number of characteristics with the cockatoos. They have a moveable crest, coloured ear patches resembling those of some of the cockatoos, and the female is barred on the breast and tail. Both sexes share incubation and the newly hatched young have yellow down. Both cockatiels and cockatoos hiss when threatened.

(Above, right and overleaf)

Cockatiels, *Nymphicus hollandicus*, are small crested parrots which are related to the cockatoos. They are friendly and affectionate little birds and consequently are popular as pets. The sexes are markedly dissimilar, the male having much more yellow on the face and crest than the female, which is mostly grey except for yellow barring on the tail. Cockatiels, which are also called quarrions, are birds of the interior. They inhabit open country, usually not far from water. They usually lay five eggs in a hollow limb or a tree trunk, most often in a eucalypt.

Cockatiel, *Nymphicus hollandicus*.

TYPICAL PARROTS

Members of this group are robust, medium-sized parrots with short tails. They are brightly coloured and the sexes are markedly different in appearance. Tropical rainforest is their usual habitat. Only two species occur in Australia, in the rainforests of Cape York—the red-cheeked parrot and the eclectus parrot.

The eclectus parrot, *Eclectus roratus*, is a stocky parrot with a large bill, a short square tail and smooth, glossy plumage. Its range includes the New Guinea region and the east coast rainforests of Cape York in northern Queensland.

Sexual dimorphism in the eclectus parrot is so striking that the male and female were at one time thought to belong to different species. The male is predominantly green with a yellow-tipped red bill. The female is mainly red with a blue abdomen and underwings, and a black bill.

LONG-TAILED PARROTS
These parrots are medium-sized or large birds, usually with strongly contrasting plumage colours. They show marked sexual dimorphism.

King parrots are primarily birds of forests and woodland, and are usually seen in pairs or small flocks. They feed on fruits, berries, nuts and seeds, as well as on blossom, nectar and leaf buds.

With his scarlet head and underparts, and pale green wing stripe, the male king parrot, *Alisterus scapularis*, is a striking sight. The female has a green head, throat and upper parts, and a red abdomen and lower breast.

Red-winged parrots, *Aprosmictus erythropterus*, occur in open woodland and scrubs, and along tree-lined watercourses in northern and inland eastern Australia. The female is less brilliantly coloured than the male, being mostly grass green, with a narrower red band on the wing.

Red-winged parrots nest in a hollow branch or tree hollow, usually in a eucalypt close to water. For some time after they leave the nest, the young birds stay with the parents in a family party. The young male shown here will not attain full adult plumage until he is more than two years old.

GENUS *POLYTELIS*

Parrots in this genus are restricted to mainland Australia. They are medium-sized birds with long, graduated tails. They have long, pointed wings and relatively small bills, which are either red or coral coloured.

Regent parrots, *Polytelis anthopeplus*, occur in two populations, one in the south-west of the continent, and the other in south-western New South Wales and northern Victoria, along the Murray River and in adjacent mallee habitats. The bird illustrated here is a male. The colouring of the female is much more subdued, being mostly olive green. This species has suffered from loss of suitable habitat and nest hollows, resulting from land clearance and the destruction of old trees in logging operations.

There is a marked difference in colouring between the male and female superb parrot, *Polytelis swainsonii*. The male is the bird with the yellow face and throat, divided from the green breast by a red crescent. The female is subtly coloured, mainly in shades of green.

The princess parrot, *Polytelis alexandrae*, was named for Alexandra, the Princess of Wales, who was later to become Queen Alexandra. This lovely parrot is also known as the rose-throated parakeet.

Princess parrots are infrequently observed in the wild, and little is known of their biology. This is hardly surprising, as they are nomadic and inhabit arid areas, far from water, in western central Australia. Because of their beauty and friendliness, and their ability to breed well in captivity, they are popular as aviary birds.

(Right)

The seeds of the marri, *Eucalyptus calophylla*, are a major food source of the red-capped parrot, *Purpureicephalus spurius*. These birds are rarely seen far from marri, even preferring them as nest sites. This dependence on one species of tree, combined with its restricted distribution, make the red-capped parrot very vulnerable to loss of habitat.

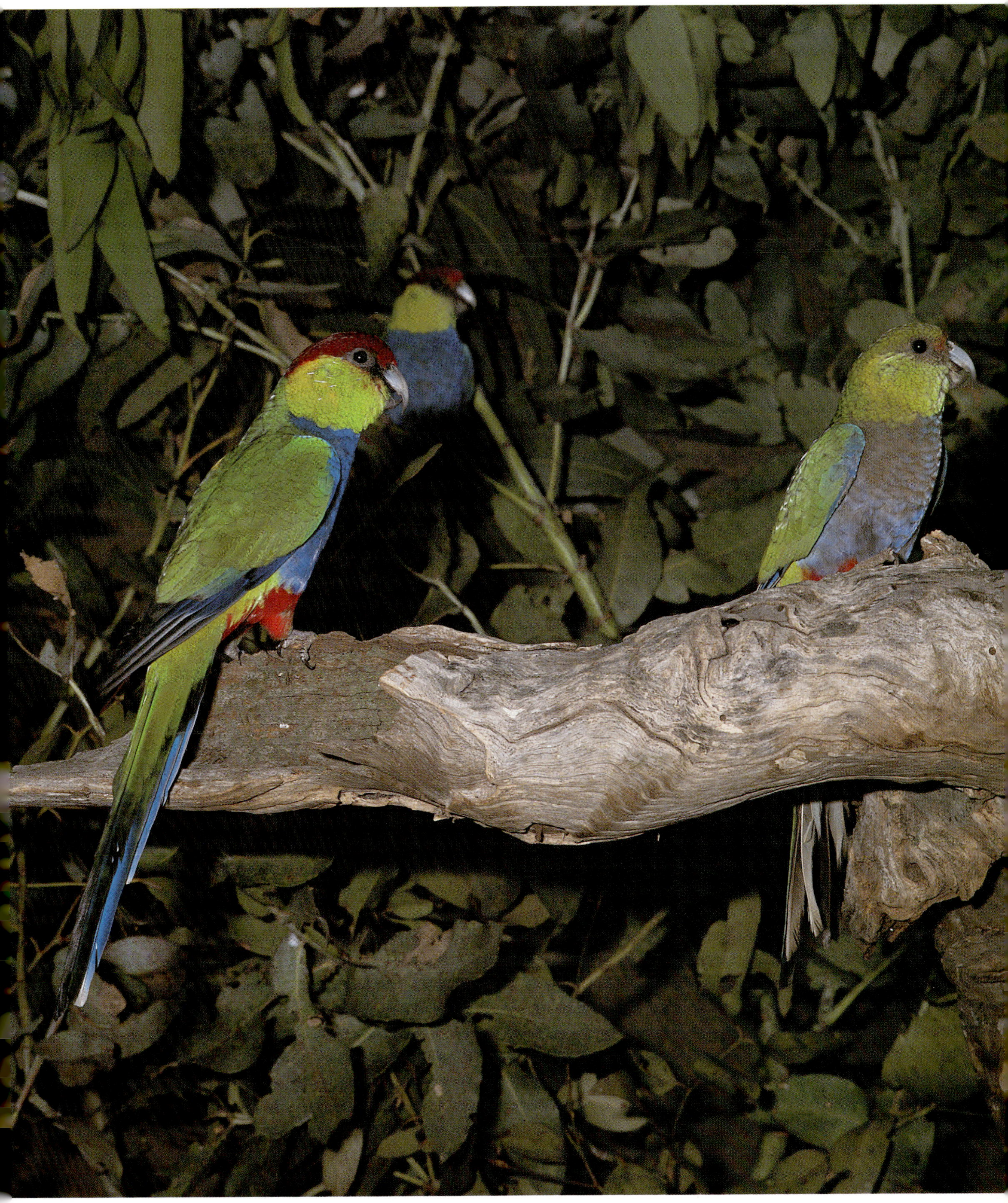

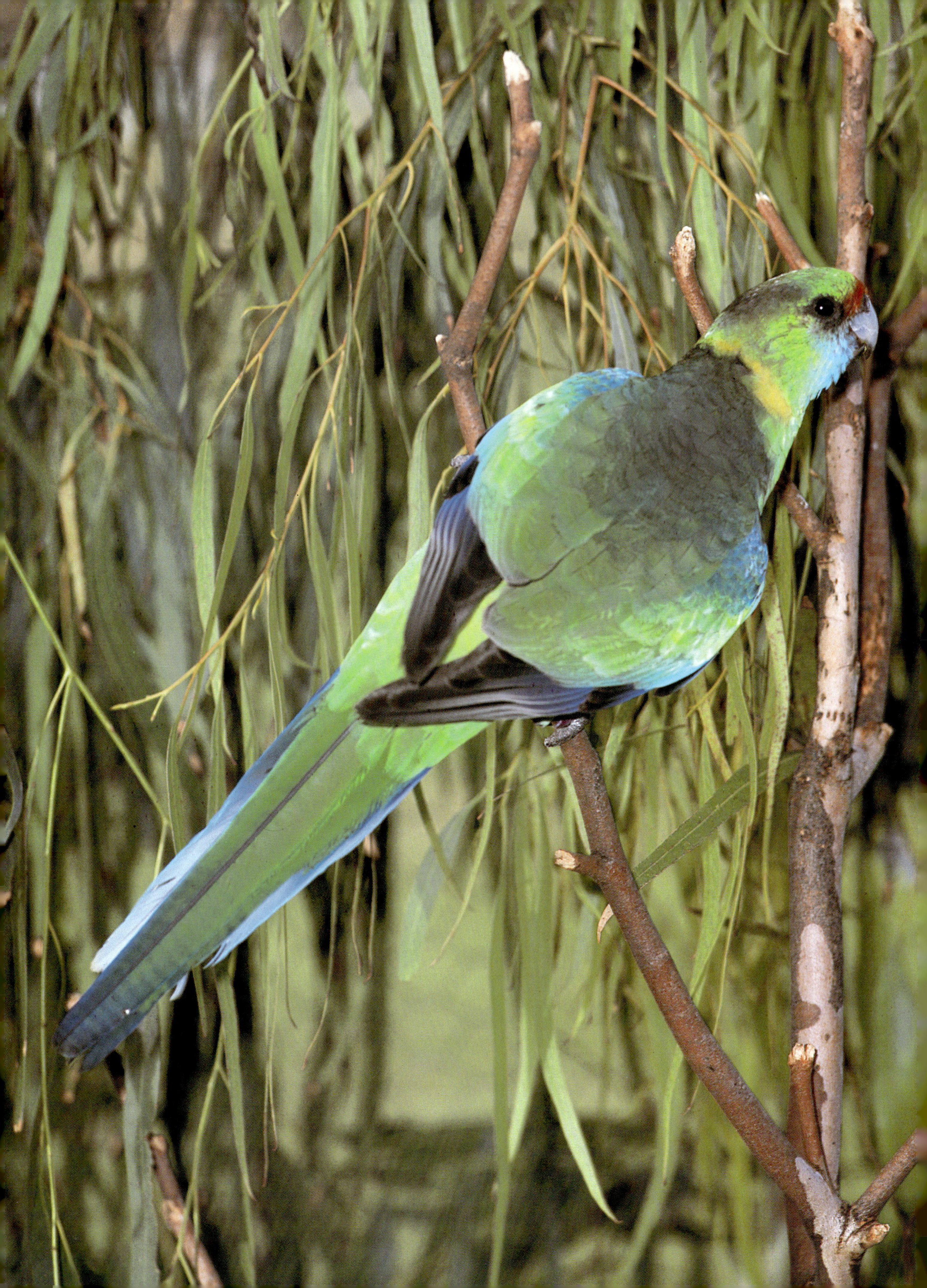

BROADTAILED PARROTS

Most of the broadtailed parrots have long, broad, graduated tails. Their bills are small, and may be black, grey or horn-coloured, but are never red. In most cases, plumage differences between the sexes are only slight. The ringnecks and rosellas are members of this group.

GENUS *BARNARDIUS*, Ringnecks

Ringnecks are closely related to rosellas. They are distinguished by their narrow yellow collar, and have indistinct cheek patches and no mottling on the back. They occur in several geographical forms, which hybridise where their ranges overlap.

(Left and below)

Mallee ringnecks, *Barnardius barnardi*, are birds of scrubs, including mallee, open woodlands, and timber along watercourses. Their range extends through the eastern inland from north-western Queensland to southern New South Wales, north-western Victoria and eastern South Australia. They nest in a hole in a tree, most often a eucalypt, or in a hollow limb. Five eggs are usually laid. The female does all the brooding, only leaving the nest in the morning and evening to be fed by the male.

Port Lincoln parrots, *Barnardius zonarius*, subsp. *zonarius*, are distributed throughout central and south-central Australia mainly in timbered habitats. The normal contact call is described as a repeated, whistling 'kwing-kwing'.

The twenty-eight parrot, *Barnardius zonarius* subsp. *seimtorquatus*, is very closely related to the Port Lincoln parrot. It differs in the pronounced frontal band, larger size and the heavier bill. Its voice is also different. The tri-syllabic contact call resembles 'twenty-eight', hence its common name.

GENUS *PLATYCERCUS*, Rosellas

Rosellas are distinguished by their well-defined cheek patches and the mottled pattern of their backs. There are two groups of closely related species within the genus:

The green, crimson, yellow and Adelaide rosellas all have blue-violet cheek patches and juvenile plumage which is mainly green.

The other group, made up of the eastern, pale-headed and northern rosellas, have white cheek patches and young which resemble their parents in colouring.

One species, the western rosella of south-western Australia, is different from both these groups, having yellow cheek patches and marked colour difference between the sexes.

The name rosella is thought to be derived from Rosehill, a suburb of Sydney. 'Rosehill parakeet' was the early common name for the species now known as the eastern rosella.

Green rosellas, *Platycercus caledonicus*, are restricted to Tasmania, some of its offshore islands and the larger islands of Bass Strait. High moorlands and deforested farmlands are the only habitats not frequented by this species, although it prefers sclerophyll forests and savannah woodland. The berries of the introduced hawthorn provide a favourite food resource for green rosellas, particularly in winter.

Crimson rosellas occur in humid forest habitats, from sea level to high mountains. Two populations occur, one in eastern and south-eastern Australia from south-east Queensland to southern Victoria, and a second in north Queensland from the Eungella Range, near Mackay, to the Atherton Tableland.

(Right)
An adult crimson rosella alights at its nest hole in the trunk of a eucalypt. Between four and seven eggs are laid, and the female alone incubates them for nineteen days.

Four crimson rosellas, *Platycercus elegans*, feed on the ground. This habit is characteristic of the whole rosella group. The diet of crimson rosellas includes seeds, fruits, berries, nuts, buds, nectar and insects. They also eat the fruits of ornamental plants and cultivated fruit such as apples and pears, so that they sometimes become a nuisance in orchards.

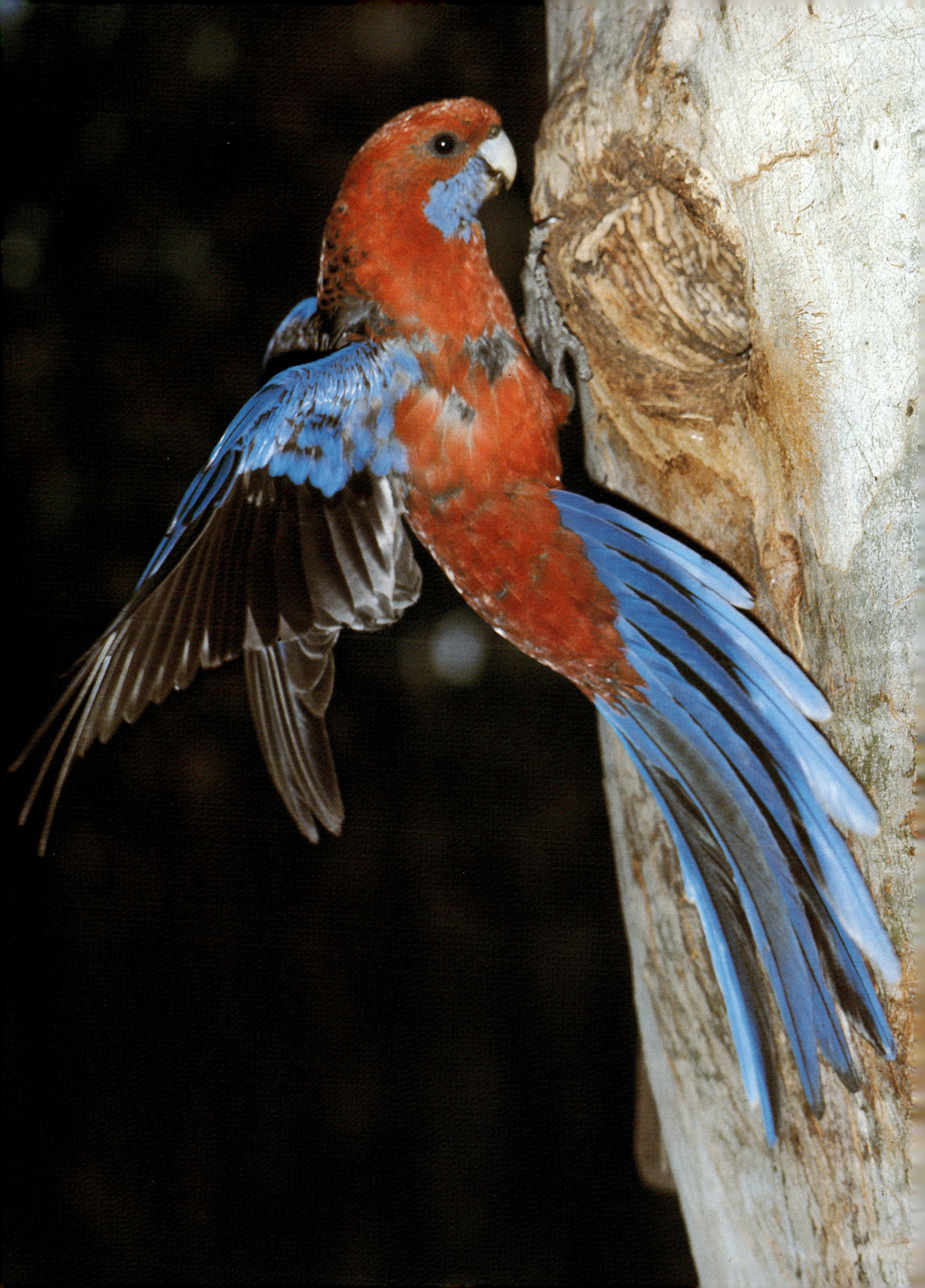

The colourful eastern rosella, *Platycercus eximius* subsp. *eximius*, occurs from central eastern New South Wales to the south-east of South Australia. It frequents woodlands, open forests, farmland surrounded by trees, and timber along watercourses. It is also a familiar visitor to parks and private gardens in towns.

An immature crimson rosella feeds on the ground. The predominantly green plumage of young birds and the blue cheek patches are characteristic of this group of rosellas.

As their name implies, Adelaide rosellas, *Platycercus elegans* subsp. *adelaidae*, occur in the vicinity of Adelaide. They have a restricted distribution, from Clare in the north, to the tip of the Fleurieu Peninsula in the south.

Adelaide rosellas inhabit a variety of timbered environments. Adults are usually seen in pairs or in groups of up to five, while young birds may form wandering flocks.

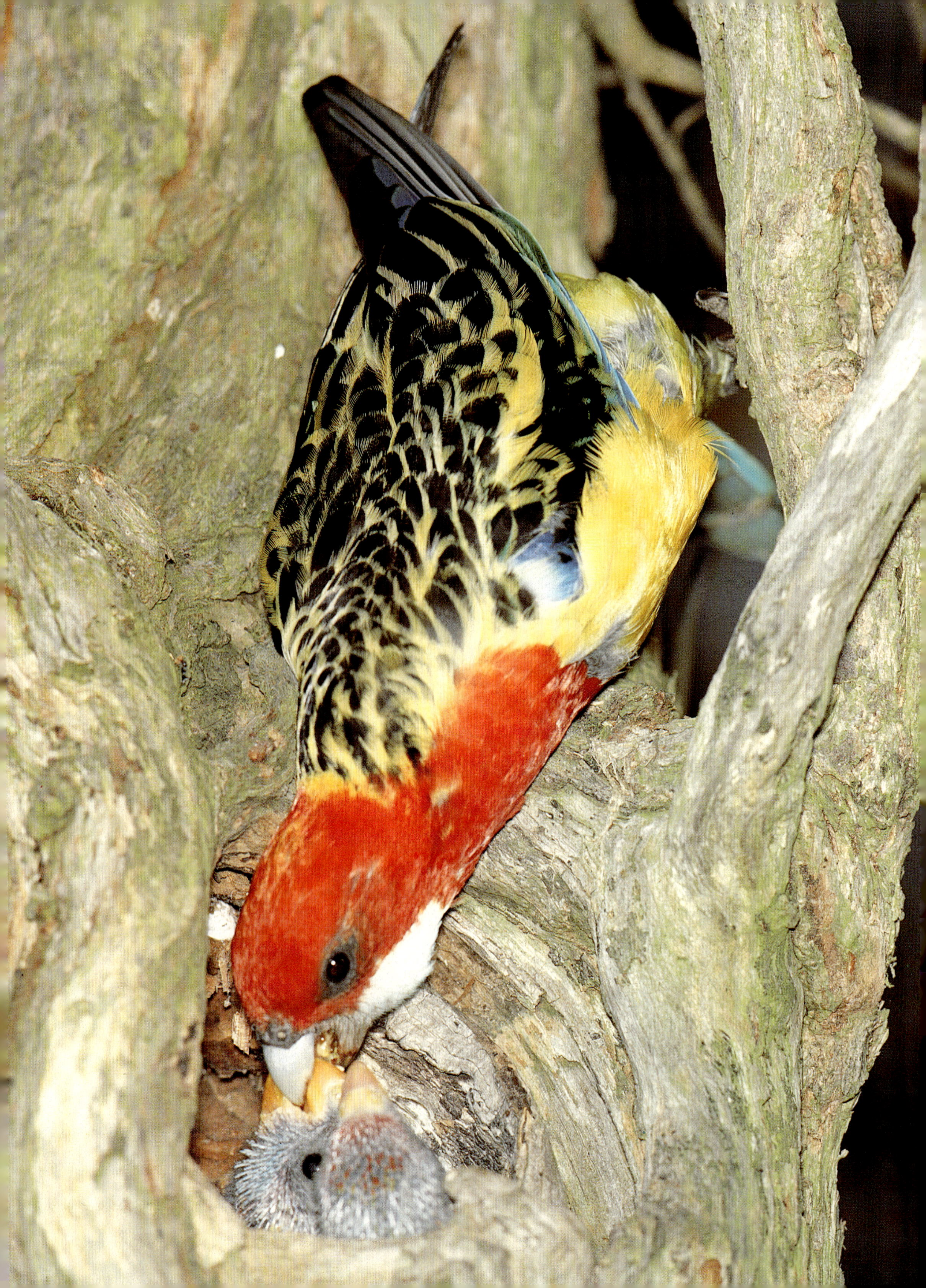

The golden-mantled rosella, *Platycercus eximius* subsp. *cecilae*, is a subspecies of the eastern rosella, occurring from south-eastern Queensland to the Hunter River valley in New South Wales. It is distinguished from the eastern rosella by its darker red head and breast, and by its back feathers, the margins of which are broader and gold in colour, rather than yellowish green.

Immature golden-mantled rosellas do not reach adult colouring until they are at least one year old. Unless a second brood is raised, the young birds remain with the parents in a family group.

(Left)
Eastern rosellas usually nest in tree hollows, but may use a fence post or tree stump. The chicks are fed by the female until they are about ten days old, after which both parents share the feeding.

The pale-headed rosella, *Platycercus adscitus*, is closely related to both the eastern and northern rosellas. It is a lowland species which occurs in eastern Australia from the Cape York Peninsula south to the Clarence River in New South Wales.

These rosellas inhabit scrub and woodland, timbered watercourses and farmland adjoining these areas. They are usually observed in pairs or small parties, often feeding on or near the ground.

(Right)

The northern rosella, *Platycercus venustus*, is a handsome bird, with its black cap, white cheek patches and blue shoulders and tail. Its breast feathers are pale yellow edged with black and the undertail coverts are red. Its range is in northern Australia from the Kimberley region to far north-western Queensland. It is an uncommon bird and is usually seen in pairs or small groups of six to eight birds.

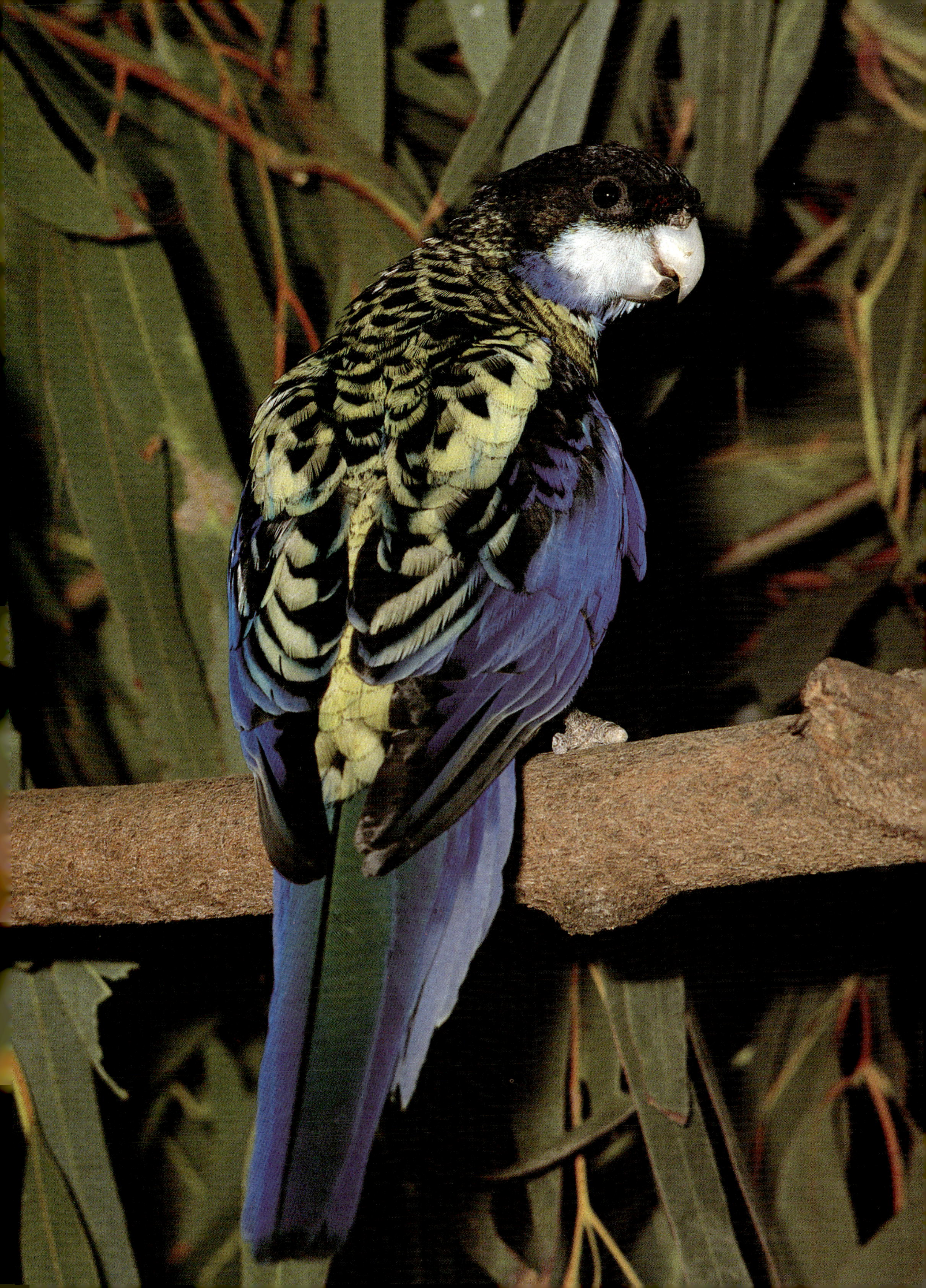

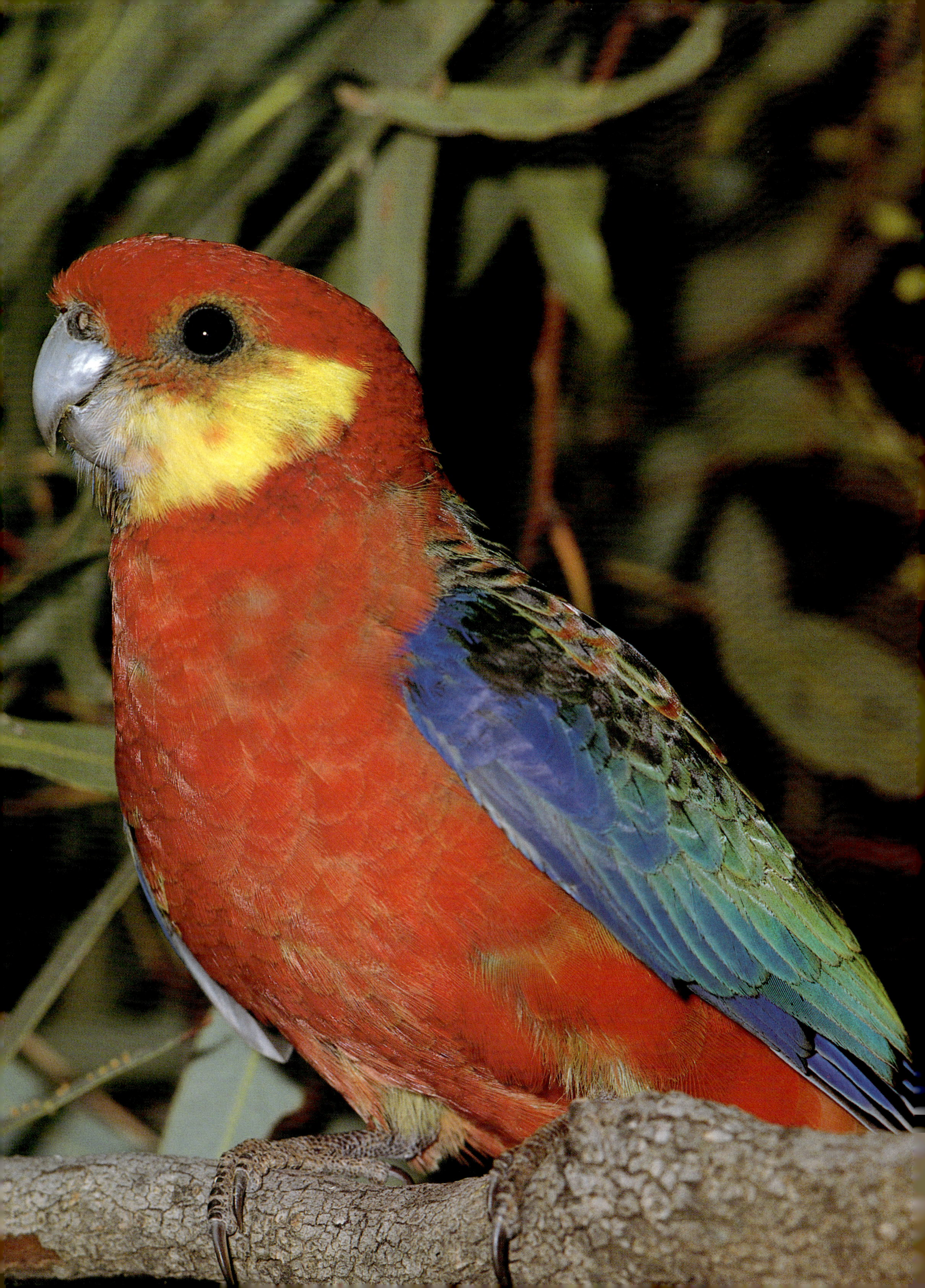

(Left)
The smallest of the rosellas, the western rosella, *Platycercus icterotis*, is confined to the south-west of Western Australia. It prefers open wooded habitats, including timbered watercourses, farmlands, orchards, roadsides and gardens.

Western rosellas are the only rosellas to have a yellow cheek patch. They also show quite marked sexual dimorphism, unlike others in the group. The female is generally darker than the male, with more green on the back, and blue edges to the outer tail feathers.

GENUS *PSEPHOTUS*, Grass Parrots

Parrots in this group, which includes the red-rumped parrot, bluebonnet and mulga parrot, are slim, medium-sized birds. Their backs are uniform in colour and they have long, graduated tails. All except the bluebonnet show marked sexual dimorphism. They are all ground-feeding seed-eaters.

One member of this group, the paradise parrot, is thought to be the only species of Australian parrot to have become extinct since European settlement.

Female red-rumped parrots are less colourful than the males, and do not have red on the rump. Nests are usually in a tree hole or hollow limb, often in a eucalypt close to water. More than one pair may nest in the same tree.

Red-rumped parrots, *Psephotus haematonotus*, are common in lightly timbered habitats throughout their range in south-eastern Australia. They are seldom far from water, and may be seen in woodlands, timber along watercourses, grassland, farms, mangroves and urban parks.

Grasslands, arid scrub and groves of trees scattered through sandy plains are the types of habitats favoured by mulga parrots, *Psephotus varius*. Their range in the interior of southern Australia extends from central and southern Western Australia to western New South Wales and south-western Queensland. The male mulga parrot has a yellow frontal band and shoulder, and a scarlet patch across the belly and thighs. The female is generally green in colour, with red on the nape and shoulder.

Unlike other members of their genus, bluebonnets do not exhibit very pronounced sexual dimorphism. Members of this species are able to raise their blue frontal feathers to form a small crest, as shown in the photograph.

Red-vented bluebonnets, *Psephotus haemaatogaster* subsp. *haematorrhous*, are inland birds. Their range extends from Texas and Milmerran in southern Queensland to the black soil plains of the middle reaches of the Namoi and Gwydir Rivers of northern New South Wales.

(Right)

Male and female hooded parrots, *Psephotus chrysopterygius* subsp. *dissimilis*, are markedly different, the male with a rich yellow wing patch and a black cap, and the female coloured mainly in soft shades of green. These birds, which depend on terrestrial termite mounds for nesting sites, are restricted to the north-eastern region of the Northern Territory.

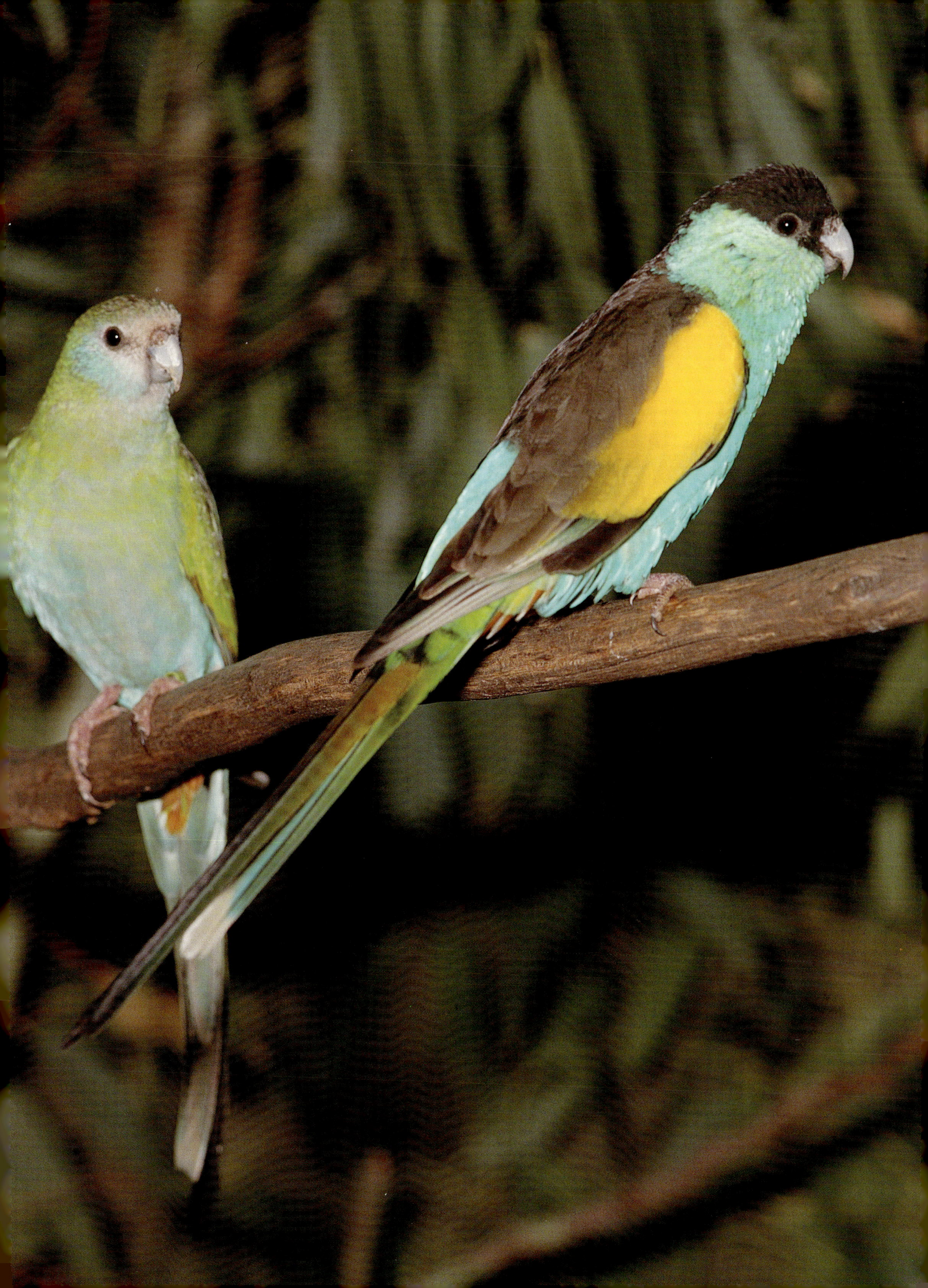

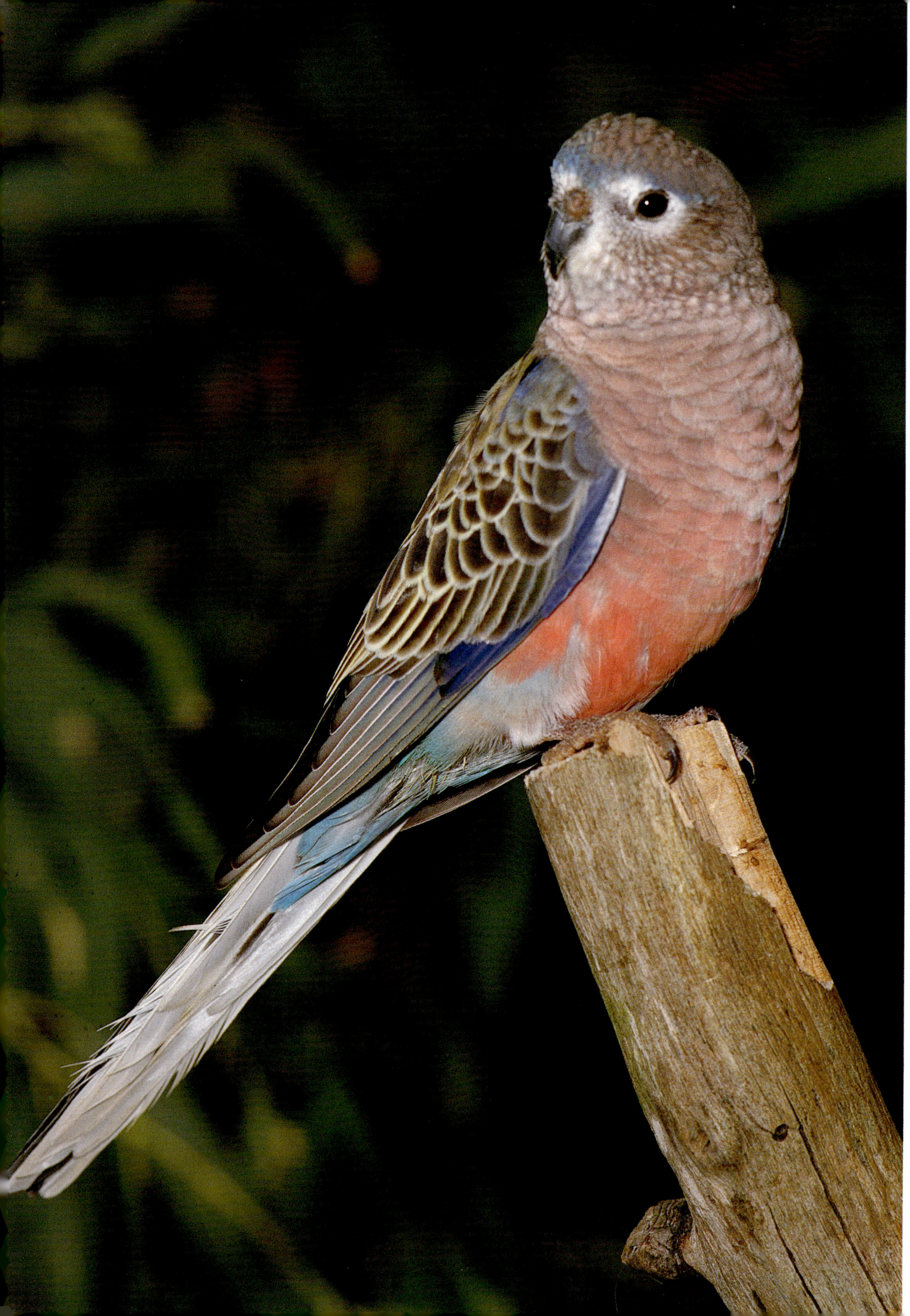

GENUS *NEOPHEMA*, Grass Parrots

Members of this genus are small ground-frequenting birds. They are graceful parrots which fly swiftly in a darting, zig-zag manner. Apart from Bourke's parrot, which is predominantly soft brown and pink, they all have plumage which is mainly olive green in colour.

(Left)
Bourke's parrot, *Neophema bourkii*, is a nomadic bird of the arid and semi-arid scrubs of the inland, particularly those dominated by mulga, *Acacia aneura*. Its range lies generally south of the Tropic of Capricorn, from south-western Queensland and the north-west of New South Wales, to Western Australia.

Blue-winged parrots, *Neophema chrysostoma*, are found in south-eastern Australia, including Tasmania and islands in Bass Strait. They frequent a variety of habitats, including open woodlands, lightly timbered grasslands, coastal scrub, heaths, coastal dunes and saltmarsh. This species breeds in Tasmania, southern Victoria and the south-east of South Australia. In autumn, most Tasmanian birds migrate north to spend winter on the mainland, returning in late spring. They may travel as far as eastern South Australia, north-western New South Wales and south-western Queensland.

Arid scrublands, particularly mallee and mulga with a spinifex understorey, are the habitats favoured by scarlet-chested parrots, *Neophema splendida*. Their range extends across the southern interior of Australia, from south-eastern Western Australia to the Flinders Ranges in South Australia, and south-western Queensland. The subdued plumage of the female is in sharp contrast to the bright colouring of the male shown in the photograph.

(Left)
Turquoise parrots, *Neophema pulchella*, were once abundant in New South Wales and Victoria, but their present distribution centres on south-east Queensland and northern New South Wales. Their range and numbers have declined, as a result of loss of suitable habitat, and also from illegal trapping for aviculture. The bird shown here is a female. The male has more blue on the face, is bright yellow underneath, and has a red flash on the wing.

GENUS *LATHAMUS*

The only member of this genus, the swift parrot, *Lathamus discolor*, has a rounded cere, a small bill, long, pointed wings and a 'brush' tongue. The sexes are very similar in appearance. Swift parrots are considered to be most closely related to members of the genus *Psephotus* and the rosellas. The brush-like tongue of this species has evolved independently from that of the other group of nectar-feeding specialists, the lorikeets.

Swift parrots, *Lathamus discolor*, occur in timbered habitats in eastern and south-eastern mainland Australia and in Tasmania. The entire population breeds in Tasmania. In March and April, most of the birds travel north to the mainland, where they spend the winter. While some birds travel as far as the mid-north coast of New South Wales, southern Victoria is their main wintering area.

GENUS *MELOPSITTACUS*

The budgerigar, *Melopsittacus undulatus*, is the only member of this genus. These parrots, Australia's smallest, have long, graduated tails and swift, erratic flight. They feed on the ground, mainly eating the seeds of grasses and herbs. Budgerigars are restricted to mainland Australia, occurring in drier regions, often in large flocks.

In the wild, budgerigars occur in only one plumage, which is predominantly green and yellow. In captivity, however, numerous other colour forms have arisen through selective breeding.

Index

Numerals in *italics* denote photographs.

Adelaide rosella (*Platycercus elegans* subsp. *adelaidae*) 43, 47
Alisterus scapularis 10, 11, 13, 15, 34,
Aprosmictus erythropterus 9, 35

Barnardius 40–2
Barnardius barnardi 40–1
Barnardius zonarius subsp. *seimtorquatus* 42
Barnardius zonarius subsp. *zonarius* 41
black cockatoos 7, 10, 13, 17, 21, 22, 23
blue-winged parrot (*Neophema chrysostoma*) 9, 10, 11, 59
bluebonnet, red-vented (*Psephotus haemaatogaster* subsp. *Haematorrhous*) 56
Bourke's parrot (*Neophema bourkii*) 9, 17, 58, 59
breeding 16–17
broadtailed parrots 41–53
budgerigars (*Melopsittacus undulatus*) 9, 11, 16, 62

Cacatua galerita 8, 13, 26, 27, 28
Cacatua leadbeateri 9, 15, 28–9
Cacatua roseicapilla 9, 10, 11, 13, 16, 17, 24, 25, 26
Cacatua sanguinea 6–7, 9, 17
Cacatua tenuirostris 8, 30
Callacephalon fimbriatum 14, 17, 24
Calyptorhynchus funereus 13, 21
Calyptorhynchus funereus subsp. *baudinii* 17, 22, 23
Calyptorhynchus magnificus 7, 10, 23
cockatiel (*Nymphicus hollandicus*) 10, 16, 17, 31–2
cockatoos 7, 8, 9, 10, 13, 14, 15, 21–30
communication 14–15
corellas 6–7, 8, 9, 17, 30
crimson rosella (*Platycerus elegans*) 15, 43, 44–5, 46

eastern rosella (*Platycercus eximius* subsp. *eximius*) 43, 46, 48, 49
Eclectus roratus 10, 12, 33

features
  bill and tongue 8
  colour 9
  feet 8
  plumage 10
  sexual differences 10
  feeding 12–13

galah (*Cacatua roseicapilla*) 9, 10, 11, 13, 16, 17, 24, 25, 26
gang gang cockatoo (*Callacephalon fimbriatum*) 14, 17, 24
Geoffroyus geoffroyi 12, 33
Geopsittacus occidentalis 12
Glossopsitta pusilla 19
golden-mantled rosella (*Platycercus eximius* subsp. *cecilae*) 9, 17, 49
golden-shouldered parrot (*Psephotus chrysopterygius*) 12
grass parrots 54–62
green rosella (*Platycercus caledonicus*) 43

ground parrot (*Pezoporus wallicus*) 12, 13, 14, 17

habitats 11–12
hooded parrot (*Psephotus chrysopterygius* subsp. *dissimilis*) 12, 56, 57
hookbill parrot *see* red-capped parrot

king parrot (*Alisterus scapularis*) 10, 11, 13, 15, 34

Lathamus discolor 8, 12, 61
little corella (*Cacatua sanguinea*) 6–7, 9, 17
little lorikeet (*Glossopsitta pusilla*) 19
long-billed corella (*Cacatua tenuirostris*) 8, 30
long-tailed parrots 34–9
lorikeets 7, 8, 9, 10, 11, 12, 15, 18–20

Major Mitchell cockatoo (*Cacatua leadbeateri*) 9, 15, 28–9
mallee ringneck (*Barnardius barnardi*) 40–1
Melopsittacus undulatus 9, 11, 16, 62
mulga parrot (*Psephotus varius*) 17, 55

Neophema 9, 10, 11, 12, 17, 58–60
Neophema bourkii 9, 17, 58, 59
Neophema chrysostoma 9, 10, 11, 59
Neophema petrophila 12, 16
Neophema pulchella 60
Neophema splendida 60
night parrot (*Geopsittacus occidentalis*) 12
northern rosella (*Platycercus venustus*) 50, 51
Nymphicus hollandicus 10, 16, 17, 31–2

pale-headed rosella (*Platycercus adscitus*) 50
palm cockatoo (*Probosciger aterrimus*) 9, 12, 14, 17
paradise parrot (*Psephotus pulcherrimus*) 16
parrots
  broadtailed 41–53
  grass 54–62
  long-tailed 34–9
  typical 33
Pezoporus wallicus 12, 13, 14, 17
pink cockatoo *see* Major Mitchell cockatoo
Platycercus 8, 9, 11, 13, 15, 17, 43–53
Platycercus adscitus 50
Platycercus caledonicus 43
Platycercus elegans 15, 43, 44–5, 46
Platycercus elegans subsp. *adelaidae* 43, 47
Platycercus eximius subsp. *cecilae* 9, 17, 49
Platycercus eximius subsp. *eximius* 43, 46, 48, 49
Platycercus icterotis 52–3
Platycercus venustus 50, 51
Polytelis 9, 36–9
Polytelis alexandrae 9, 37, 38
Polytelis anthopeplus 9, 36
Polytelis swainsonii 9, 36
Port Lincoln parrot (*Barnardius zonarius* subsp. *zonarius*) 41
princess parrot (*Polytelis alexandrae*) 9, 37, 38

Probosciger aterrimus 9, 12, 14, 17
Psephotus 12, 16, 17, 54–7
Psephotus chrysopterygius 12
Psephotus chrysopterygius subsp. *dissimilis* 12, 56, 57
Psephotus haemaatogaster subsp. *haematorrhous* 56
Psephotus haematonotus 17, 54
Psephotus pulcherrimus 16
Psephotus varius 17, 55
Psitteuteles versicolor 15, 20, 21
Purpureicephalus spurius 13, 38, 39

quarrion *see* cockatiel

rainbow lorikeet (*Trichoglossus haemadotus*) 7, 11, 15, 18
red-capped parrot (*Purpureicephalus spurius*) 13, 38, 39
red-cheeked parrot (*Geoffroyus geoffroyi*) 12, 33
red-rumped parrot (*Psephotus haematonotus*) 17, 54
red-tailed black cockatoo (*Calyptorhynchus magnificus*) 7, 10, 23
red-vented bluebonnet (*Psephotus haemaatogaster* subsp. *haematorrhous*) 56
red-winged parrot (*Aprosmictus erythropterus*) 9, 35
regent parrot (*Polytelis anthopeplus*) 9, 36
ringneck, mallee (*Barnardius barnardi*) 40–1
rock parrot (*Neophema petrophila*) 12, 16
rose-breasted cockatoo *see* galah
rose-throated parakeet *see* princess parrot
rosella (*Platycercus*) 8, 9, 11, 13, 15, 17, 43–53

scaly-breasted lorikeet (*Trichoglossus chlorolepidotus*) 18
scarlet-chested parrot (*Neophema splendida*) 60
sulphur-crested cockatoo (*Cacatua galerita*) 8, 13, 26, 27, 28
superb parrot (*Polytelis swainsonii*) 9, 36
swift parrot (*Lathamus discolor*) 8, 12, 61

Trichoglossus chlorolepidotus 18
Trichoglossus haemadotus 7, 11, 15, 18
turquoise parrot (*Neophema pulchella*) 60
twenty-eight parrot (*Barnardius zonarius* subsp. *seimtorquatus*) 42

varied lorikeet (*Psitteuteles versicolor*) 15, 20, 21

'wee juggler' *see* Major Mitchell cockatoo
western rosella (*Platycercus icterotis*) 52–3
white-tailed black cockatoo (*Calyptorhynchus funereus* subsp. *baudinii*) 17, 22, 23

yellow rosella 43
yellow-tailed black cockatoo (*Calyptorhynchus funereus*) 13, 21